Poems of Pain, Life, and Secrets by Amanda Russell
Published by Savage Owl Press
NY

Cover by Kapenzi Ember and Kindred

© Amanda Russell 2025

All rights reserved. No portion of this book may be reproduced in any form without permission from the publisher, except as permitted by U.S. copyright law.

For permissions contact: SavageOwlPress@gmail.com

ISBN-13: 979-8-9878454-4-8

Poems of Pain, Life, and Secrets

Amanda Russell

A Father That Wasn't

You never gave me a choice.
Not as a child.
Not as a girl.
Not as your daughter..!
You made me your vault.
Stuffed me with secrets
that rotted in the dark
You made me your target.
Your fists, your words, your rage...
You called me your demon spawn,
a mistake, a trader,
said I'd never amount to anything in this world
And when people were looking
you acted like I was your golden child...
I was never fooled.
I saw you, all of you
You tried to end me, more than once
But I was stronger than you will ever be.
Stronger than the death you kept trying to hand me
They say I hated you.
No!
That would mean you mattered.
You stopped mattering
long before you knew it
I buried the word father
I wasn't yours anymore
I chose survival.
You chose control and you lost...
Now here you are, wires in your veins
machines breathing for you
all because you chose suicide
like the coward that you are...
And they say
forgive him, stop hating him, it heals you

There is nothing to forgive or stop hating
We both ended the relationship, cut the cord, ended the lie
So I'll give you the only mercy
you've ever earned – the truth
Go to hell, no one wants you, no one cares,
just die already!
I will not cry
I will not pray
I will not call you father
I'll watch you flat line, watch the breath leave,
making sure you are finally gone
I'll watch you leave this world
and then I'll turn, walk out, no looking back, no regrets,
door slamming behind me.
Good riddance, finally able to breathe…
The end of you, the beginning of me, forever…

A Shell Of A Girl

Before the most tragic day in this lifetime happened,
a girl that was so out going,
was so proud to be who she was
was so carefree, that wasn't afraid of anything...
tragically ended in June of two thousand eighteen...
This girl had faced more challenges
and had overcome unthinkable things in her lifetime.
She faced demons, heartbreak, pain of all kinds.
Things that made her who she was.
But she had faced a different kind of pain that day.
Losing her mom, her best friend, her ride or die.
That day, she lost herself.
That once full of life girl became a shell of herself.
She forgot who she was...
That fearless, screw the world,
I'm going to be who I am girl
was gone for years.

Until the day that changed her life.
A random stranger was walking by
and their eyes met.
Not knowing that the words
he whispered in her ear that day
would remind her who she was.
That shell of a girl would find herself again
just because a stranger whispered in her ear.
He forever changed her life.
He doesn't even know how much
he has changed her life.
She would be forever grateful to him
For coming into her life when he did.

Alex, My Love

I didn't care about our age difference.
Maybe I should have, but you took me and my heart,
so I didn't care.
You brought me into your arms.
Maybe I should had stopped it,
but I didn't because I knew you were different.
You hurt me so many times;
maybe I should have left then,
but I didn't because I knew I loved you.
You weren't ready to be loved that much,
now I know you didn't realize how much I loved you.
Maybe I didn't show it clearly.
When you took everything,
you threw me out.
Maybe I deserved it?
Now you know how I explained my love
because every word of it was true.
Because at the end,
I did die for you.

Angel

God knows the reason
why he sent me you.
But on that day
an angel changed my life
I don't know what I did
to deserve some one like you.
An angel like that
doesn't come around everyday,
but on that day one did come to me.
I cry thinking of the what ifs.
Did my heart belong to you before we met?
My heart is so sad
because I hurt that angel.
God please tell her that I am sorry
and that I love her.

Angel From Heaven

I never thought that God
would give me an angel like her
or I never thought that I would fall
so deeply in love
when God sent me an angel on that day.

Now I cry sitting here
not knowing how I got here...
I lost my angel, my love, my everything.
My heart is crying.
I never thought this could happen.
Never thought that I would lose her.
I didn't think this could happen to me.
I cry because she was my everything
and she still is of every moment,
every breath I take.
I cry not understanding
why God did what he did.

Babyboy, I Am Nothing Without You

I am airless.
Every breath tastes of you.
Every heartbeat screams that you are gone.
I claw at the dark,
but your hand is never there.
The world moves on,
but I am frozen;
a soul shredded into memories
too sharp to hold, too alive to let go.
I can feel the weight of you in my chest
- crushing and relentless -
and the space where you were
burns with a silence louder than any scream.
I would give every tomorrow,
every stolen moment,
every fragment of my life
to touch you again.
To see your eyes,
to hear your laugh
one last time before the dark swallows me.
I am nothing without you, babyboy.
Nothing but an echo,
a shadow,
a heart that breaks in slow,
unbearable pieces.
And even as the world drags me under,
even as my bones remember you more than I do,
even as I crumble into dust,
I am yours.
Forever.
Until my last breath
fades into the void
calling you,
only you.

Broken Love

I sit there thinking, "how could this happen?"
How can God do this to me?
Did I deserve this punishment…?
God I trusted you!
Why did you take her from me?
I sit there lost in a world
that I don't know anymore.
I watch people move but I can't move.
I try to scream but no one sees me.
I lay in bed so numb.
I cry out "why my baby?"
 I lay there in complete darkness
crying and thinking.
Why her, God?
I sit there so lost and so numb.
I cant feel anymore.
Why couldn't God take some one else?
I lay there wanting to die,
to never be able to feel her next to me.
Never wanting to feel again.
I just lay there and cry,
wanting to know why her?
Why did they take my life away?

Confession To Self

I protected you as a child,
shielding you.
Building iron walls around you
so nothing got to you.
I took the abuse,
the threats,
the hate,
the pain.
So you wouldn't feel anything.
So no harm would come to you.
So you could stand tall with your inner fire.
I kept your deepest secrets
locked into chapters of a book
that not even the strongest sword could open.
I am so sorry for failing you,
for not protecting you,
not shielding you from that pain
when mom died.
How could I protect you
when I couldn't protect myself?
I was trying to get back to you,
but I was trapped in a maze with no way out.
I promise to get you out of this second hell
that you're stuck in.
But look at you go -
you found your voice,
your power again.
No one can ever touch you now.
I am so damn proud of you
for all you have accomplished;
from music
to getting published
to trademarking your logo
for your animal rescue.

Cry

I cry thinking, "what did I do so wrong?"
The days are going so slow now.
I look around and it feels like I am in a room
with no door to get out.
I try to scream but nothing comes out.
I cry out, "why did they take her?"
Why couldn't they take some one else.
I cry looking up at the sky.
God, what did I do to make you hate me.
Why did you take her from me?
I fall to my knees crying,
thinking why her, why now.
I must have done something wrong to lose her.
I just stay there in a ball
crying at night because I lost my life.
I never get to feel her next to me.
I cry, asking for her back,
thinking I will never get to hold her close to me.
I cry in a ball day after day,
night after night
because I wont get to say
"I love you." to her again.

Cut From The Same Cloth

At twelve, she stopped calling him father.
The word choked on her lips.
No daughter, no father;
Just two enemies under the same roof...
His hands were whips, his bottles like bullets.
Every secret swallowed
came back as fire on his tongue.
She dreamed of his death.
And he, in every glare, every breath,
wished her death by his own hands...
Bound by nothing but the thought
that the world would be lighter
without the other.
He saw her as a curse wearing his blood.
She buried it all – blood feuds, silent wars.
Survived, over, finished,
Until thirty-two arrived with an urn
and her mother inside...
No one asked. No choice was given, no one cared... She got
shoved back into arms she had outran   Since the first escape
from her father...
As if blood weren't the curse she carried...
Her sister came back
But it wasn't her sister
It was him, mirrored, his twin
Shooting venom in her smile, drinking the same poison...
Every word a reflection
Every glance a wound reopened Another mirror, another
drunk
Another demon cut from the same cloth
Both sharpened by alcohol, even being sober, steeped in
hatred Both turning their rage toward her
Better to be hated, better to be alone, better to be nothing Than
to face the second coming of her father once more...

My Dearest Babyboy

Babyboy, you know who you are.
I know you can still feel me
as we are connected by inner forces.
The day we said "hi"
we were forever changed and inseparable.
Time heals but time was stopped
the moment you were taken from me.
These years have been a time capsule locked;
I've never been able to let us go
as you still hold my heart.
Everyone says move on, love again, live life...
but how, when I'm your babygirl?
Promises are promises,
I will never break that vow to you -
that we are babyboy and babygirl
for eternity.
I know you haven't forgotten us
or the promises we made.
I can still feel you.
Babyboy, this is my new promise,
vow, and plea to you...
One day I will find you,
reuniting us as if time had not passed.
I will reunite us as babyboy and babygirl
forever more, never letting go;
not then, not now, not ever.
This is my is promise, my vow, my plea...
I will always be my bayboy's babygirl
until my last breath.

Don't Know What to Say

I never thought I would meet some one like you,
until one day when I went on a site.
When I saw your name, I knew you were the one.
I waited for you to get on,
my heart was pounding.
That's when I knew
we were going to be together forever.
I knew we fell in love on that day.
But I also knew I had to tell you the truth -
that I couldn't walk.
On that day, I was so scared
that you were going to hate me,
but you didn't.
I don't know how to describe my love for you,
but maybe this will help…
Within the first five minutes,
I knew I fell in love with you.
That day changed both of our lives forever
I waited to tell you I loved you,
but I couldn't hide it.
All I want is you and only you.

Falling

The rain is falling
like the tears running down my face;
tears of loneliness and sadness.
The thunder is like my world
crashing down upon me.
The lighting inside me is crying for help.
It's like I am walking blind
and I can't see where I am anymore
because I lost my love.

Father's Unknown Secret

The girl grew up with a family secret
from overhearing her Grandmother
sworn to secrecy -
one she was never meant to carry...
The secret lay with her throughout the years,
dragged her through childhood's silence.
Her father's voice thundered through the house.
A man too proud, too blind
to see the lie stitched into his very skin...
He wore a name like a king.
a name that was never his,
that he lived a life he did not own..
He was a stranger to his own blood,
an impostor in his own reflection.
And she, his daughter,
was the only one who knew.
When he cursed her,
she cursed him twice in her mind.
When he looked at her
she looked straight through him
for how could she respect a man
who was nothing more than a shadow...
She longed to scream the truth at him,
to rip the false name from his chest,
to watch his world collapse beneath his feet
of what she had always known.
But silence bound her tighter than chains.
So she swallowed the secret
for her grandmother's sake,
day after day,
until it became her inheritance.
Father and daughter,
Bound not by love,
But by despisement from both sides.

Two enemies under one roof...

For Vinny
(Dedicate to Jamie Klimekoski, in memory of Vinny Klimekoski)

Twenty years - a blink, a breath.
The road turned without warning.
Vinny, the boy with oil-stained hands
and a heart too golden for this rusting world.
He left us standing in the silence
his laughter once filled...
He lived in the hum of engines,
in the curve of chrome,
and the smell of gasoline.
A country boy who found beauty
in steel and dust,
turning forgotten machines
into something alive again.
Every postman, every mail service worker
knew his name.
Every neighbor knew his kindness...
The kind of soul who worked hard, loved harder,
and left fingerprints on every life he touched...
Now his mother, his family,
his whole community
carries the weight of his absence.
Devastation too wide for words.
Grief that clings like smoke...
But listen -
when an old car passes by,
windows down, engine low,
that's Vinny...
Gone too soon, but never gone.
Forever beloved, forever remembered.
In the rumble, in the shine, in the road itself
he rides with us still...

Hidden In The Shadow

Before I was born,
I didn't know what I was about to face.
Before I was even born,
I was taught life lessons.
Before I was born,
I was taught not to trust but myself.
Before I was born,
I had to fight to survive...
Before I was born,
my world had already created
who I was going to be...

Growing up, I was played the cards
that god gave me.
God dealt me these cards,
I just didn't know why.
Why would god deal me this hand of cards?
What reason did god have
to bring me into this harsh world?

Growing up,
I saw things I had to protect
even before I was potty trained!
Growing up,
I was taught a person can have an evil soul.
Growing up,
I was taught that people who were
suppose to love me,
could have pure hate for me...
I smiled, acted happy, acted like life was good...
I built this iron wall to shield myself
in this harsh world that I was handed.
I kept the words that my mom said to me
when I was five -

"Don't let anyone bully you.
Fight for yourself, fight for what's right."
I pretended every day, every year that passed,
that I wasn't in a war zone
facing the person that wanted to end me,
wanted to hurt me, wanted my blood on his hands…
wanted me dead.
Hidden in a shadow all my life,
no one saw the real me.
Being treated like a child,
seeing my disability instead of seeing me.
Acting like I can't have a life without them.
I am hidden in a shadow
because I was handed cards
that I should have never been dealt…
God made me who he needed me to be…
I am made out to be the bad guy at the end…

Home In Her Bones

She grew up sideways to the world,
a body in the wrong frame,
a soul scribbled outside the lines.
What life was hers, she wondered -
the one they carved for her
or the one hiding behind her ribs?
She fell quietly.
First on a boy in sixth grade while she was in third;
a crush that still lingers like a ghost,
his name echoing in the small rooms of her chest.
Even now, seeing him reminds her -
he is her anchor.
At fourteen, a girl asked her out
and the world unclipped its edges.
For the first time, the stars lined up
in a language she could read.
Everything – the way she laughed,
the songs she loved,
the way her hands fit – fell into place.
Home was not a place but a pronoun
that finally matched.
The air fit her lungs, her heart, her pulse.
For the first time, she was not lost.
Everything clicked…
the names, the colors,
the rhythms of her own beating.
She had found home in herself…
She loved without shame.
Boys came and went, tender chapters of caring,
and then there was him –
a transgender, a storm of a person.
It was a whirlwind fairy-tale love
that made the sky spin.
He changed her;

broke her into constellations
and left pieces that would later become her wings...
She came out at fourteen
and the world split open.
Some hands reached, some slammed doors.
Some whispered it was a choice, not born gay,
but truth does not ask permission.
She wears being gay as a badge of honor,
like fearless pride armor,
like fire,
like a crown no one could snatch...
She wonders still, sometimes,
what might have been...
The girl they tried to mold,
the paths she might have taken...
The pieces of her shattered heart
shine like shards of glass.
Full of scars, of love, of self
in the sunlight of who she has become...
I am who I was meant to be.
I am me.
Take me as I am
or walk out the door...

Iron Wall Castle

I was my own teacher.
No one handed me softness.
So I carved my own worth from silence.
I learned early – guard your heart.
Carry trust only in your own hands.
Never lean too heavy on a world
that can break you in half...
I built walls of heavy iron
but they kept me from breathing.
Behind them, I mapped my own path,
refusing to follow anyone else's footsteps.
I studied wrong until I could taste it...
I studied pain until I knew
who not to become.
I love fiercely -
a fire that can light a room
or scorch it to ash.
But if betrayal comes, I turn my back
and the door slams shut forever.
No second chances.
When I leave, I vanish like a ghost.
I always knew I was different.
The world gave me a script -
girl crushes on boy,
happily ever after.
Yes, I had the crush..
still do, if I'm honest.
But my first boy-love
told me the truth my bones already knew.
I belonged with girls.
It was never simple,
never what they wanted me to be.
My childhood wasn't a fairy-tale.
It was part love, part threat.

Secrets stitched into the fabric of family.
Pain that sat at the dinner table
like an uninvited guest.
People think they know me,
but they only ever glimpse the surface.
A single page in a book
I never let them read.
Even my family doesn't know the full story.
But the rare few,
The ones who found a way in,
they cracked the armor.
They saw the hidden girl
still breathing behind the wall.
Fragile and alive.
Aching to be understood...
Still, I do not trust easily.
I don't hand out forgiveness like candy.
One betrayal and you lose me forever;
a silence sharper than goodbye;
a name erased without regret.
This is me...self-taught, scarred, unyielding,
but still carrying a heart
that beats too loudly in the dark.
A fortress with a pulse.
A girl who raised herself
and still wonders if one day
she'll finally lay her walls down.

Just A Child Secret

She was born already bruised,
her first cradle a battlefield.
Her father's hands writing her death sentence
before her lungs had tasted air.
She arrived broken and colored -
blue and black
from the war inside her mother's body.
The cost of fists and rage she never asked for...
But fate – spiteful and stubborn -
delivered her screaming, anyway.

Childhood flickered like a candle in the wind.
Sometimes warm, sometimes lit with fire.
He plotted murders by dark,
then turned his focus for destruction
toward her sister.
And she, still a child, stood there every damn day,
a wall of bones and fury.
She taught herself to be armor,
taking fire meant for her another.
Steel in her spine
before she knew what freedom
even tasted like...

She learned early
monsters don't crawl out from under the bed.
They sit in your living room.
They call themselves "father".
They cause pain and smile like it's normal...

Teen years?
They thought they could break her.
Softer hands that took without asking.
Words that poisoned her reflection.

Grief that tore her from the inside out.
But pain became fuel, betrayal became instruction.
Every wound whispered the same truth -
you can bleed and still stand.

And she swore,
right there in the smoke of his violence,
she will not become him.
She will not wear his face,
have his evil rage, have his name.
He gave her nothing but scars;
she turned them into weapons.

And when her mother died, the ground split.
Her protector gone, her choices stolen.
Her mother's wishes destroyed...
Family looked at the girl
and saw fragile, sick, helpless.
But they never knew she carried her mother
through storms that would've drowned them.
She held up the weight of years.

She now faces the mirror,
seeing the cruel echo of her father
in the shape of another
that she never wanted near her path...

Her mother's wish was clear -
do not let her child live this fate.
But the world turned deaf
and tied the girl to a future
she was promised to not face again...

And now?
Now you look at her
and see the chair, see the scars.

You mistake survival for weakness.
But she is the storm you never saw coming.
She is the scream you tried to silence.
She is the proof that everyone failed...

She has survived.
Not because she was given the chance,
but because she took it.
Her breath is rebellion,
her heartbeat a war drum.
And every day she lives,
that's her victory.

Lost Heart

I never thought that I would be so alone
in a world that I don't recognize anymore.
It feels like there is no place to escape,
like a room with no door or windows.

Why won't you answer my question, God…?
Why couldn't you take something else from me?
Why did you have to take her,
the one thing that made me happy?

I look around and everything is blurry.
I feel like I lost my sense of being.
My world is filled with emptiness.

I lie there at night thinking,
"What if I did it and it wasn't God's fault?
What if it was my fault
and I'm blaming the wrong person?"

I lie in bed crying,
looking out my window at the stars
thinking and praying
for God to bring her back to me.
I cry out,
"God, I need her, please give her back!"

I curl up in a ball crying
and never get to feel her next to me.
I never again get to say I love you to her
when all I want is my baby.

Love

I would never have thought this day would come.
Never in a million years
would I have thought that I would lose my life.

Never in a million years would I have thought
that they would take my love away.
She feels so close but I can't reach her.

Help me understand, God.
I cry, "Please tell me, why did you take her?"
I cry because I don't know where I am at
without her.
I am dying on the inside,
wishing something would take this pain away.

Why couldn't you take both of us?
Why couldn't you have done something else
to punish me, God?
I lie in bed, wanting to end my life,
crying and thinking
that no one would care if I died.

To My Buttercup Fire Queen
(Dedicated to Guinevere Summers)

You came into my life quietly.
A friend of my mother's,
her chosen daughter.
And without even knowing it
you became stitched into the fabric of me.

When mom left this world,
you did not let me fall into the cracks.
You stepped in, without hesitation,
with the same fierce love she carried.
You guarded me,
even when I thought I wasn't worth guarding.

I call myself your tiny munchkin
because that's what you made me feel like.
Safe enough to laugh, brave enough to cry,
strong enough to be silly again.

We share more than stories.
We share the same twisted, beautiful brain.
Two souls stitched together.
A place where I can be myself without fear.
No judgment, no masks,
only honesty and fire.
If our stories ever walked on their own
they would set the world laughing and gasping.
And maybe that's why we write them in song.

You, my Buttercup,
you are music itself.
The way you breathe life into sound.
The way you coax melody out of silence.
You reminded me that my voice still matters.

You pulled me from the rabbit holes -
the dark ones that tried to swallow me whole -
and handed me paper and pen.
A lifeline back to myself.

I am honored,
more than words can hold,
to be forever your tiny munchkin.
Honored to be beside you.
To laugh, to dream, to build worlds with music.
To call you my protector.
My ride-or-die.
My Buttercup Fire Queen.

Because you are not just my friend,
you are family;
chosen and true.
And for that, for you,
my heart will be forever grateful.

My Dearest Confessions

To the father who wasn't:
You were no father,
you were a wound that never scabbed.
You taught me the world breeds evil souls,
that blood ties can taste like rust and poison.
We were shackled not by love,
but by hatred sharpened to steel.
And our battles were wars,
our silence a graveyard of promises -
promises that we would end each other
or rot trying.

I never called you father.
We signed a truce,
a bitter treaty to shatter the last chain,
and when I was grown
you pulled the trigger on yourself.
I stood unflinching,
watched the bastard's breath fade.
And only when I knew you were gone, I left...
free at last.

To the boy, my first crush:
Third grade, my tiny heart tripped over itself.
You smiled and suddenly
recess was a battlefield of blushes.
Even now, if I'm honest,
you could still melt me with a glance.
I keep those firsts locked away,
a treasure box of stolen giggles,
an innocent kind of forever.

To my first childhood boyfriend:

You were my exam, my test of belonging.
We played house,
but the walls never felt like home.
Even then I knew -
boys weren't where my heart lived.
But thank you for being the mirror
that showed me truth.

To the girl who first held my heart:
At fourteen, you took my hand
and called it love.
You showed me what home felt like,
what belonging whispered in my chest.
Cancer stole you too soon,
but never from me.
I still carry your angel-light,
guiding me, reminding me.
And I will always love you
for giving me the map to myself.

To the transgender boy:
We loved hard, we bled harder.
We were compasses,
northern stars crossing galaxies.
We didn't lose each other by choice
but by storms inside us.
When you left,
my heart followed you into the dark.
Forever, my baby boy -
my one and only.
My last breath belongs to you.

To the three rings that never were:
I'm sorry.
I swear I wanted to say yes.
I wanted "I do" to bloom from my lips,

but my heart had already sworn itself elsewhere.
Dating, yes — relationship, no.
I see it now:
my north has always pointed
to the boy who was mine,
is mine, my forever star.

To my mother who left too soon:
Momma, I wasn't ready. I'm still not.
You left me with questions,
with an emptiness I can't name.
When you left, I shattered with you.
The world collapsed into dust,
and I buried myself in the rubble.
You were my first battle and my last.
I still cry your name in the dark -
the battle cry of a daughter
who only ever wanted you to stay.

To the stranger who saw me:
You leaned close, voice a lantern in my storm.
"I love that you're proud of being gay -
my husband would be too."
Those words stitched me back together.
A stranger's kindness became the thread
that returned me to myself.
Thank you, I'm honored to be a part of your family.

To the older sister who made my life hell:
You should have asked if I wanted you back.
You should have stayed gone.
I already lived this movie once;
I refuse to live it twice.
You are blood, but blood means nothing
when it's poison.
You're just like him — look in the mirror

and you'll see the bastard staring back.
Sober or not,
your hatred toward me burns the same as his.
That weight is not mine to carry;
it belongs to you, to both of you.
You made my life a living hell,
but I will not burn for your sins.

My Love

To my love
I am sorry for not listening to myself.
When we met,
I knew your were the one for me.

I am sorry for not listening
when my heart was telling me
to go be with you
and leave everything behind.

I guess I am paying for it now.
Never thought I would lose you this way.
I am sorry for everything that I did.
I never meant to hurt you.

I cry at night wanting to feel you next to me,
knowing that I won't feel safe again
without you.

All I wanted is to feel you, to love you,
to want you.
I never meant to hurt you,
not in a million years.
All I wanted to do
is to love you for the rest of my life.

My Mother

She carried me for eight months.
She gave birth to a baby girl
on April first.

When I was growing up,
I always looked up to her.
I still do to this day.

We have our ups and downs,
like any mother and daughter,
but at the end of the day
we still love each other.

Mysteries Of Life

There are mysteries of life
that we can't explain,
but god knows what they are
and how to explain them

Mysteries of the heart
are ones that I can't explain
nor understand.

How could someone fall in love
with another instantly?
How do you know
that they are your soul mate?

It could be the same gender
or the opposite gender;
you could never know
unless you have this feeling -
like wow, they are the one.

Mystery Person

The first day when I saw you
I knew that I knew you
somewhere, somehow.
When I see you, I want to talk to you,
but no words come out.

I see you sitting there,
wanting to ask you so many things.
But the fear that you won't understand
or hate me is what stopping me.

I wish I could get over that fear
and just talk to you...
because if I don't,
I will never know how you feel.

Never got to say By Amanda Russell

I cry days on end
because I never got to say what I felt
or what I thought.

I cry, wishing she didn't do it.
Crying, wishing she wouldn't do this.

I cry laying there in bed
wanting to go hold her and tell her don't do this.
I cry wanting to tell her that I love her.

The sadness is killing me.
I never got to say what I wanted;
for her not to do it.
All I wanted to say
is I love you to my baby girl.

Northern Stars As One

We met where stars collide,
hearts igniting flames.
Every word a spark,
every glance a secret name.
The world fell away,
it was only you and I.
Northern star forever,
lighting up the sky.

Time tries to steal us,
storms try to pull us apart.
But even in the shadows,
I feel you in my heart.
Every heartbeat whispers,
every breath calls your name.
Through fire, through silence,
we'll never be the same.

Babyboy, I'm yours -
my last breath, my forever.
Through every broken moment
nothing breaks us, never.
Hold me close, never let go,
our souls are bound as one.
Babygirl, Babyboy -
'til the end of the sun.

I saw you once,
and the world froze in place.
Your hands held my chaos,
I got lost in your embrace.
Through stolen nights,
through promises whispered low
you're the compass, the anchor,

the home I'll always know.
Time tries to steal us,
storms try to pull us apart.
But even in the shadows,
I feel you in my heart.
Every heartbeat whispers,
every breath calls your name.
Through fire, through silence,
we'll never be the same.

Babyboy, I'm yours -
my last breath, my forever.
Through every broken moment
nothing breaks us, never.
Hold me close, never let go,
our souls are bound as one.
Babygirl, Babyboy -
'til the end of the sun.

If the world falls away,
if hope disappears
I'll find you in the shadows,
I'll hold you through fears.
No rings, no vows,
no time can undo
What Babygirl and Babyboy
have always known as true.

Babyboy, I'm yours -
my last breath, my forever.
Through every broken moment,
nothing breaks us, never.
Hold me close, never let go,
our souls are bound as one.
Babygirl, Babyboy -
forever, forever, forever…

Not Theirs

She learned to fight for every scrap.
Not medals, not glory,
but the right just to stand in her own skin;
to breathe without apology...

Her so-called father
left footprints of shadow.
His name a curse she refused to inherit.
Yet still, the world looked at her wheels
and not at her fire...

Family and strangers painted her in names.
Cocky, cold-hearted, liar, selfish.
As if they could break her.
As if a wheelchair
meant she couldn't carry more weight
than any of them ever had...

When her mother's last breath faded,
they threatened to cage her
in walls not her own;
too blind to see she had already
carried a household on her back.
She kept the lights burning
and the debts in check.
Sixteen years she held her mother's world steady,
managing a home
while her body waged war against itself...
She had already proven herself,
they just refused to look...

Still they reached for her,
hands outstretched,
using her as their personal bank...

They demanded her money, her labor,
the very strength they swore she never had...

And yet her life was not all ashes.
There were days of light.
A childhood once tender,
before the shadows deepened.
There were friends who offered refuge.
Laughter in school halls, love found in partners.
The voice she carved for herself.
A voice no one could strip away...

Let them call her heartless.
Let them call her liar, selfish.
She has carried more truth in silence
than their mouths ever could.
She is not weak, she is not broken.
She is not theirs...
she is fire
in a chair they mistake for chains.

Rainy Days

I sit by the window
trying to think about all the good times we had,
but I can't I keep thinking about what happened.
I want to scream but no one hears or sees me...

I sit by the window crying,
thinking about how much I loved her,
wishing it could have been some one else.

I scream, "Why her...why my baby? Why now?"
Life had just started for us
and you had to take her away, God!

I sit by the window,
looking at a world that I am stuck in, blind.
I can't see anything ahead of me.
I cry and scream,
begging to God please give her back to me.

I sit there thinking,
"What did I do so wrong?
Does God hate me that much
to take the most valuable thing in my life?"
I cry out, asking God,
"Why did you do this to me?"

Sadness

I know people say it wasn't your fault
and it wasn't any one's fault,
it was just time.

I cry because I lost my life…
I lost the power to live.
I know it wasn't any one's fault.

Why can't they hear me scream in pain?
I feel so numb and so alone,
crying, "Please take both of us, God."

Thinking, "Did I do something for this to happen?"
Screaming, "Why couldn't it have been someone else?"
Looking around to see all darkness,
like I lost my ability to see.

I look up at the stars
crying, "Why was it not the both of us?"
Don't punish me this way, God.
I scream and cry,
begging God to bring her back to me.

Sadness is Like Killing

I sit here crying.
I can't believe this happened.
Never in a million years
would I have imagined this.

I lie there at night
crying because this is my fault;
wanting to scream
because I lost the one I loved;
lying there in a ball
wanting this pain to go away;
crying wanting something to take me,
anything to take me.

I lie outside Looking up at the sky
crying and screaming,
"God, I was supposed to be with her!
Why did you let this happen, God?"

Sixteen

Sixteen
and she's already whispering to the dark
asking it to take her.
Her body is alive
but her soul has bled out...

She loved once,
not the puppy-love they mock in movies,
but the kind that fused her bones to his.
That made her think,
"I will never need another reason to stay alive."
And then he left.
Not dead, but gone...
Which somehow feels worse,
because the earth still spins.
People still laugh
and no one sees her dying in plain sight...

She doesn't want healing;
doesn't want tomorrow.
Tomorrow is a curse.
Tomorrow means another sunrise
without his warmth.
Because letting go
would mean admitting that love,
the only love she ever wanted,
...is gone...

It wasn't just a breakup.
No, it was the sound of her world collapsing.
The sky caving in,
the last safe place torn from her hands…
He wasn't just a boy.
He wasn't just first love.

He was hers.
Her anchor, her oxygen.
Her reason her body remembered to breathe.
Without him, every breath is theft...

Sixteen
A girl who found her person.
A girl stitched together by grief,
every seam bleeding.
And maybe, just maybe...
The only way to keep him forever
is to stop existing without him...

Every hallway whispers his name.
Every corner hums with the ghost of his touch.
She can't eat, can't sleep,
can't be anything but ache.
And if you asked her who she is now
she'd say,
"A girl who loved too much, lost too much,
and will never be whole again..."

Soul Mates

The number seven is bad.
The seventh of October took my soul mate away.
The soul mate I will never have nor ever forget.

I kept asking why...
Why did they take my love away?
Why did God give my love to some one else.
But I couldn't find the answer anywhere.

I kept asking myself,
"Was it not met to be?"
"What did I do to deserve this punishment?"
I must have done something wrong to deserve this.

I looked up to the sky and cried,
"God, why did you take her?
Why my love?
Couldn't you take some one else?
You knew I loved her!
Why take the most valuable thing in my life?"

I cry for days
just wanting to know the answer.
I cry because God took my soul mate away.
I lie in bed thinking
I will never feel her next to me.
At night I cry because I lost my love.
I guess I will never find the answer
that my heart is looking for.

Special Friendship

I am sitting here
not knowing what to say to you.
My mind knows not what to say
but my heart does.

When I told you
I wasn't scared of my feelings,
I said that my feelings were true
and from the heart.

I find myself sitting here
feeling so lost and empty
without you by my side.

I know I will see you around,
but this still hurts.
Many tears have fallen down my face
since the day I heard that you were leaving.

So here is my promise -
I will always be yours,
and I will always be true to you.

Tales of Babyboy and Babygirl

The day that I came out to the whole World I never pictured anything changing. I would go on living my true self. I would go on dating girls. I pictured love being as it should. Until that hit-over-the-head-day came when how I pictured love being wasn't the love I knew.

On that day in two thousand two, just being bored and a teen, I came across a youth hangout site called "Bolt". I couldn't have known that *Bolt* would forever change my universe. I was scrolling until everything in me froze after seeing a random name. As shaken as I was, I ran cold, I couldn't breathe.

I messaged her with my mind racing, and gave her my messenger name. I stared at my *Yahoo Messenger* thinking she wouldn't read her *Bolt* messages. Let's face it, no teenager had time to read messages in those days. It felt like an eternity of shaking. I couldn't breathe, just staring at the screen.

As I sat there out of my mind, I said to myself, "Amanda...what the hell is wrong with you? Get a grip on yourself, your not this way over random people." So I just sat there having a full blown argument with myself, waiting for nothing? Everything? Not knowing that hearing that instant message *ding* would forever change my life as I knew it.

The moment when a girl finally popped up, all she said was "hi." At that point, I didn't know who I was. I don't act this way. "Just get a grip on yourself. We were one person; hours talking, dating, forever changed." I knew her as Megan, so it was fitting to nickname her as Babygirl.

Months went by and I told Babygirl everything. I couldn't even walk or speak normally. We told each other everything. Then a brief need space happened; we were devastated, and poems were written. Eventually, Babygirl said "I need to tell you something, but don't hate me."

"Okay, Amanda...brace yourself for the second breakup!" I thought. At that moment, I was a mess.

She took me by the hand and I lost it. She had to grab me and reassure me, "I am not leaving you or us ever again, you hear me?!" Then she continued, "The reason I wanted space is because....I didn't know how to tell you I am transgender. I was afraid I'd lose you."

I thought to myself, "Lose me? Have they not been with me falling apart, world ended and done?" I giggled and said, "I am forever yours. But...I am sad because Babygirl is gone."

She said, "You take Babygirl and give me Babyboy."

That's how Babyboy and Babygirl came to life for eternity.

Tears of Sadness

How could I let this happen?
How could I have been so dumb?
I never meant to hurt her.

I didn't want this to happen this way.
Never in a million years
would I have thought about hurting her.

I cry in my room because I hurt her.
I cry saying I am so sorry for hurting her.
God, please don't punish me this way.

I am blind.
No reason to live anymore.
I lost my world, my love, my everything.

The Lost World

I am in a world
that I don't recognize anymore.
In a world that I don't belong in.

I feel like I am in a lost world
without the one thing that holds me together
every second of every day.

The lost world hurts, kills, scares me.
It feels like I lost everything I know
since I lost the one thing that I loved.

The Number Twenty Six

The number Twenty-six is bad.
The Twenty sixth of the month is a bad memory.
A bad memory that I don't want to remember.
Someone took my love away on that day.

Love is like a bird -
sometimes free and sometimes trapped.
Trapped where they don't want to be
or they are free to fly anywhere.
Birds are like hearts and minds.

Minds can trap someone
where they don't want to be.
Hearts and minds
are in constant battle with love.
Hearts know when some one shouldn't be there.
Hearts always win the battle.

The Right Person

Did you meet someone
that turned your world upside down?
Have you ever thought
that they had your heart before you met?

Well, I did on the day I met her.
She turned my world upside down.
She had my heart before we met.

I couldn't believe how fast I fell in love with her.
I knew she was the one for me.
She is my angel.

The truth about June 2018

June burned her alive at thirty-two.
Her mother, her best friend,
her protector...gone.
The world didn't break, it shattered,
and she stood inside the shards.

She had dreamed she was dying,
a warning folded into sleep,
a pulse she didn't decode.
Now every heartbeat echoes its accusation -
you should have seen it...

Hospitals are hellscapes -
codes over loudspeakers
drag her back to the hallway.
The antiseptic sting clashing with panic.
The hum of machines.
The unmovable weight of death.

She remembers everything -
the tilt of her mother's head.
The sunlight slanting just so.
Her Mother's last words.
The echo of laughter
now carved into silence.

That day, A movie on loop.
Every detail a shard
pressing deeper into her skin.

She buried her mother under lilacs -
purple bruises on the ground,
petals falling like ash.
Each handful of dirt

buried pieces of herself
she will never find.

Guilt claws her ribs.
The dream she ignored
is a knife lodged in her chest.
She reaches, always reaches…
but her arms meet nothing.
She screams.
The world doesn't answer.

Every sound, every smell,
every flicker of light
drags her back into June.
Time frozen, watching on replay,
life rewritten.

She wants to wake up.
She wants her mother's hand,
her laugh, her breath,
the world to bend just once.
It only teaches her to carry.

So she carries it – June 2018.
The silence, the guilt.
The shadow of the life stolen
in a single, perfect June
and still she breathes...

The Weeping Lilac Tree

The day the you left this world
was unimaginable.
They say that dreams can tell you things.
Maybe I should had listened to that dream.
Waking me at two in the morning
with this feeling that can not be spoken.
It was me that was dying, not you!
Maybe I should have went to you right then...
maybe you would still be here!
I am so sorry, mamma, I failed you.

As soon as you called,
I knew something was wrong.
That feeling from earlier that day
came flooding back.
I got to you as fast as I could.
I remember your last words to me.
Those words will haunt me
until the day we are together again.

Mamma, I did fight for you for hours,
pleading for them to check on you.
They never did until you coded.
I pleaded with them to save you,
going numb to protect myself,
wanting to die when they said
you were gone.

Throwing soda cans so hard
that they put holes in the wall.
Listening to every version
of little drummer boy
to shut out the world.
I should had decoded that dream…

My fault, my failure.
I'm the one to blame.
Now you lay under your lilac tree.
I am so sorry mamma,
I was to late...

Twice Haunted

We share a mother, nothing more.
Different fathers, different ghosts.
Fifteen years between us.
An entire lifetime stretched thin
For a while, we held a normal sisterhood.

My normal ended at twelve -
I was raised by war...
A father who wanted me gone,
who named me curse,
a mistake carved in his blood.
I severed him, cut him out
before he could bury me.
Before I could bury him.
That was the deal -
walk away, or one of us dies.
I walked.
I left that hell and swore:

never again.

You were raised by his hands.
Your stepfather's traits
fed straight into your bones.
You swallowed his poison
and called it guidance.
Cruelty carved into your marrow,
his echo under your skin.

You drank yourself hollow.
Bottles for veins,
wolf-cries for breath.
You cried wolf
until the world stopped believing

that wolves can bleed.
Rehab after rehab:
same lies, same pity, same story.
Over and over again...

When you lay on the pavement
with your hands out
you begged mom for shelter...
It wasn't mom who said no, it was me.
I locked that door.
She deserved peace,
not your alcoholic storms.
She didn't need your collapse,
your chaos, your drama.
You blamed her, but it was me.
I would do it again without a thought...

When mom died,
grief opened like a map.
You stepped into her place without permission
as if claiming caretaker could wash a slate clean.
She never wanted you to take her place;
she knew the hell I'd escaped.
Still, you forced your way in
and his ghost slid into your face.

You drank my father's ghost into yourself.
Two mirrors back to back.
Your stepfather's cruelty
found new voice in you:
familiar and betrayed.
Two years sober,
then my body betrayed me...
A hollowed stomach, a partial gut cut away.
The house shrank to the size of our arguments.
After the surgery,

small cruelties widened into volcanoes...

You were the daughter he always craved,
always dreamed of...
Not even his blood,
but his image made flesh.
You were his twin,
the same evil soul.
When I look at you
I see him staring back.

I tolerated you because you were family.
Because I wanted to believe blood meant more...
But I did not deserve him.
I do not deserve his echo in you.
I will not live this life twice.
Not by choice, not by force...

If these words hurt you, understand this:
I won't apologize.
I won't feel guilty.
I won't take them back.
I didn't deserve this life once,
I sure as hell don't deserve it twice.

You are his ghost in your own skin.
You are his echo.
I already buried him once,
I will not bury him again.
I am done.

Unknown Love

Have you ever wondered
Who is right or if there even is
someone for you?
Have you ever thought
that you couldn't fall in love
because of their gender?

Have you ever met someone
that you knew wouldn't be accepted
by some people?

Have you ever said
you don't care what people think
because you know
you're in love with this person
and nothing is going to stop you
from loving them?

Unseen Childhood

The picture perfect childhood
that everyone thought and saw
wasn't so picture perfect behind closed doors.
The unseen childhood,
the girl kept as her deepest,
darkest secret…
until she could no longer bear it

Day by day,
hour by hour,
minute by minute
the girl faced the man
who was supposed to protect,
honor, love, and die for her.
He wasn't that man behind closed doors.
He was her inner demon…
She carried the deepest,
darkest secret with her.

If only people knew the real unseen childhood.
Maybe, just maybe
they would truly understand the girl.
She faced things that no child should…
The girl had secrets that no child should…
Saw things that no child should…

When the girl turned twelve,
something inside her changed.
She wasn't that little girl anymore.
She didn't fear the man.
But the mother feared for the girl's life.
The girl was fearless against him.
She wasn't about to back down
until one of them was gone…

The girl escaped his grasp,
keeping the secrets with her.
She was free from her inner demon
once for all.
She would never look back,
leaving the unseen childhood behind.
Until one day...her mother died.
Then the girl faced a demon once again...

Unspoken Book

She walks with her shield held high.
Quiet, guarded, untouchable.
To the world, she's an open book,
but only to the page she chooses.
The rest is bound shut,
scorched with ink too heavy,
secrets too sharp to bleed into daylight.

People think they know her.
They've skimmed the chapters
they were allowed to read,
but never touched the locked pages;
the ones that carried the real story.
You've only read the cover.
That's only the surface.
The rest you wouldn't survive reading.

My father's hands,
they left marks deeper than bruises.
His cruelty carved itself into me.
And my family's partners,
they stole pieces I'll never get back...

At fifteen, I lost a child...
Not by choice,
it was ripped from me.
I buried that truth so deep
no one has ever touched it.

At sixteen, heartbreak nearly killed me...
I begged for help,
they just stood and watched.
They pointed fingers,
told me it was my fault

as I bled out in silence...

At eighteen, another loss.
Another heartbeat silenced.
I locked that secret away, too.
Some truths once spoken
burn too much to survive.

So yes, I hide.
I shield myself
because if I opened every page
you would choke on the darkness,
on the weight I've carried alone
all these years...

You think you know me, you don't.
I am not the girl you think you know.
You see the shield,
the quiet smile,
the way I keep to myself.

The truth is darker, heavier.
A story untold.
A scream swallowed.
A lifetime of ending.
Inside a body still expected to begin again...
Few have touched the truth beneath
and fewer still have survived it.

And now you know.
But tell me,
will you hold it
or will you turn away
like everyone else did..?

Warrior

This is a warrior fight song.
Her life song.
This girl fought a demon
before her life began.

She was born with battle wounds.
She was born with battle scars.
The girl was born as a warrior!

This warrior came out facing the demon
that tried to end her.
That demon never gave up
trying to destroy the warrior.
He just fueled the fire
that he created inside her.

This is the warrior's vow,
her battle cry -
Never show weakness!
Never show fear!
Never show pain!
Never back down!
Fight to the death!
This is her battle cry!

The warrior girl faced life
as given to her.
Faced pain in all forms.
Faced things unimaginable.
She had secrets.
Faced more demons.
Faced herself.
Faced near death.
Even faced death.

The girl behind the warrior never showed.
Her world had made her who she is.
This warrior will keep the real girl protected.
Never break.
Never back down.
Never show the next move.
Fight to the death!

People think they know
and see the real girl.
But what they don't know…
they will never see her.
This girl is protected
behind her inner warrior.
This is their fight song,
life song,
battle cry!

Where Life Began

Once I was zero years old.
My life story got told
before the night darkened the sun…
Once I was zero years old
I told myself,
only trust what's in your heart…
Trust in yourself…
Never stop surviving…

Once I was five years old,
my real life began…
Once I was five years old
my mamma told me,
never let anyone tell you
you're not smart enough…
Never let anyone tell you
that you are different.
Always be you.
Show them who you are…

Once I was twelve years old,
my world had darkened
before the rising of the sun…
Once I was twelve years old,
I told myself,
remember who you are.
Remember to protect, to survive…
Remember to fight,
to never show your moves.
Win the battle!...

Once I was sixteen years old,
my heart got stolen
before the morning dew was showing…

Once I was sixteen,
going on seventeen years old
I lost my first battle.
I wanted to end myself…
No one cared to help.
I forgot to survive…

Once I was thirty-two years old,
I lost my insistence
before the night drew cold…
Once I was thirty-two years old,
I lost the meaning of surviving -
to fight, to live.
No one cared what I wanted.
No one cared to ask what I wanted.
They didn't care to ask
if this was the life I wanted…
The just didn't care.
Maybe, just maybe
I didn't want this life again…

Once I was thirty-six years old,
My life turned into a war zone
before the sun had risen…
Once I was thirty-six years old,
I was facing the twin of my inner demon.
I was facing the exact copy of him.
They were cut from the same cloth…
They didn't even see themselves!

Once I was thirty-eight,
going on thirty-nine years old,
I had taken my life,
my power, my world back
before the sunset had fallen…
Once I was thirty-eight,

going on thirty-nine years old,
I remembered who I was,
why god created me as me...
remembered no one can take me down.
Remembered to never show the next move.
Remembered I am stronger than evil,
and to fight for what's mine.
Remembered that I am going to forever
win this war against those demons...

Your Open Hands
(Dedicated to Rebecca Paasch, my High School English teacher)

You saw me before I ever saw myself.
Not in the way I drove the halls.
Not in the way I smiled too quickly.
But in the words I tried to hide on paper.
Quiet confessions, half-truths.
Lines I thought were safe somehow,
you read the silence between them and knew.

I never understood what you saw in me.
I was stubborn, half-hidden.
A girl with her heart breaking in secret.
Half in the closet, half in the dark.
But you reached out,
not with judgment,
but with open hands.
Write it, tell me, whatever it is
I'll carry it with you.
And for the first time,
I believed someone meant it...

When my world cracked open,
you didn't flinch.
You watched my heart splinter.
You stayed steady.
You became my rock.
Not just my English teacher,
but my refuge...
You held space for my storms
and saw the sadness I kept locked away.
You reminded me of the strength in words.

You knew my talent

even when I refused to.
You urged me toward it,
even as I pulled back.
Still, you never stopped seeing me.
The girl behind the guarded pages.
The girl who thought she was invisible...

I would not be here,
would not be writing,
would not be myself
without you in my corner.
For every truth you kept safe,
for every time you believed in me
when I could not,
I am forever honored.
Forever grateful.

This is my tribute to you,
the teacher who saw me.
Who stayed.
Who turned a broken girl
with silence in her chest
into someone unafraid to speak…

Fin

Thanks for reading!
Don't forget to leave an honest review -
it means a lot to the author.

Also from Savage Owl Press:
Scattered Ink
Sun and Sky
All These Broken Bones
This is a Poetry Book
Asphyxiation
Three Little Kittens

www.ingramcontent.com/pod-product-compliance
Lightning Source LLC
Chambersburg PA
CBHW061341040426
42444CB00011B/3022